Letters to Broken People

by Samia Fakih

"I can't believe how common this bullshit is."

Prelude

It's so hard to write this,
It threatens to engulf me.
But the alternative?

To bury my head in the sand?
I can't,
And I won't.

I won't turn away from it.
I won't look away from his mistakes,
From my mistakes,

I won't erase them with feigned ignorance.

I have to feel this,
The fire burning my skin,
The light bursting from within,

Smothered in darkness,
Extinguished,
Then exploding again,

Like a million fragments,
Shattered,
Reassembled,

Looping,
Like a record skipping,
On scratched vinyl.

Until the song ends,
Silence,
Peace once again.

Denial & Shock

Infidelity turns everyone,
Into collateral damage.

There was something you could hardly say out loud.

And suddenly I knew,
This typical morning,
That already felt a little off,
Heavy with something I didn't know the name of,
 —**was about to go to hell.**

How many hours has it been
since everything was fine?
How many hours was it
that I lived in a lie?

You were the love of my life, my true soul,
So why wasn't protecting our love the goal?
Were they worth it? Or her? Or him?
You should have known that there isn't one sin,

Not one misstep or slip, not one person you could screw,
That would make me ever stop talking to you.
The one thing that would make me leave,
Are all the lies you would dare conceive,

Like a castle, you built them up,
so very high,
All I saw was a home,
So I let out a sigh,

We lived in that castle,
It seemed repaired, brand-new,
But you kept patching the cracks,
Didn't you?

How foolish I was,
I had so much pride,
"How lucky am I, that we survived those hard times?"

Now I'm rocking myself,
But I can't stop from crying,
Knowing the castle we built,
Was based on you lying.

—**glass castle**

We break,
And everything is harder.

Showering.

Texting.

Getting water.

Left packing,

An entire relationship,
Into three bags.
—**personal histories**

Trauma is a mysterious beast.
It shoots a round of adrenaline through my body,
And my poor brain, my amygdala,
Feels the danger and the fear.

It keeps me high alert,
And I become an expert on animal instincts.
On the strategies the brain uses,
When desperate to survive.
A champion in the game of fight, flight, or freeze.

When the impossible suddenly happens,
A death, a betrayal, the ground opening up under you,
Your body has no time for emotions,
Only pumping blood to keep you awake,

Looking for the next danger,
Suddenly, it's not convinced you'll survive,
So you live on the edge of your seat,
There is no peace for days.

—biological reactions to trauma

I can come to understand this illness as it is.
For how could I ignore,
The countless stories of pain?

But that isn't a balm.

There is no magic potion,
To wash away,
How personal this is.

I'm the one who got hurt,
But It's not about me,
—it's an addiction

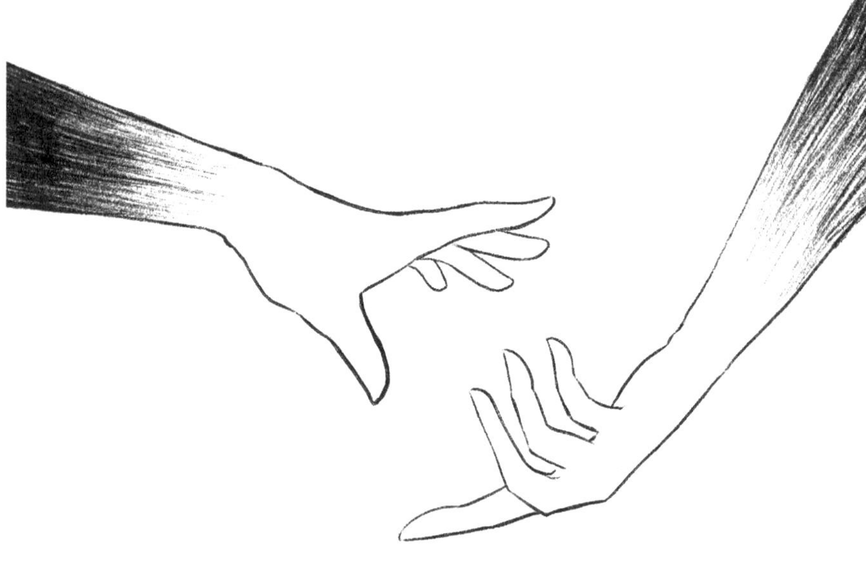

I had so many questions,
That I wanted you to answer.
I thought the truth would set me free,
But I was trapped in disbelief.

Asking again and again,
Hoping the response would be different,
I know it's ridiculous,
But I just needed a minute.

—processing, processing

"How are you?" They asked,
Gently looking at me,
Like the question mark alone,
would be enough to shake me.

They became glassy shapes as I answered.
— friends

These are the eyes that looked at me with love,
These are the eyes that avoided mine and lied.

These are the lips the kissed me,
These are the lips that told me I was imagining things.

These are the hands that caressed my face,
These are the hands that texted secrets.

These are the arms that held me,
These are the arms that held another.

These are the shoulders I fell asleep on,
These are the shoulders that gave out under fear.

This is the heart I gave,
This is the heart I was given back.

This is the one I love.
Is this the one that loves me?

—the same coin

I see how much pain you're in,
And that makes it harder to be mad at you.

So now I'm just mad.

Mad I can't even be mad.

Upset in knowing that,
        Your pain,
                was always,
                        more important.

—**I can't heal here**

Grief is like an invisible wound,
You walk around with your soul split open,
Your guts spilling everywhere,
Dizzy with blood loss,
And someone says:

"How are you?"

Because they can't see your wound,
You're left shocked, sputtering, and saddened.
You paste on a smile and reply:

"Fine, and you?"

It's the cruelest joke of fate,
That a human could be in so much
unseen pain,
Wracked with fear, sadness, rage,
Stomach churning,
Bones aching,
Chronic insomnia.

A jolt of adrenaline that keeps you awake for weeks,
Your body revolting against you,
and the pain inflicted upon you,
Trying all at once to survive any predator.

"I need sleep!"
"I need to eat!"
"I need to calm my mind!"

Your cries fall on deaf ears,
Your body no longer cares about your wants and desires,
It was your capacity for human emotion that got you into this mess,
Now it's you being thrown into oblivion.

Your body is done with you,
It's shutting you down,
You were careless,
It's time for animal instincts to take over.

Do it all for no other reason except survival.

So, you sleep when you can,
You try to eat something,
You drink water, constantly,
If for nothing more than to replenish your tears,
You sink into whatever distraction you can find,
Your soul is still screaming,
Your body vibrating,

But you look at the clock,
You've survived another hour.
The time adds up,
However slowly,
It becomes a day,

Two days,

More,

You still count them, but now there's evidence,
That you've clung to life,
That you've cocooned yourself safe from external threats,
So, your body, seeing your efforts,
Slows down just slightly,
Cools like a broken fever,
You find there is less agony each hour.

And then, one day, you look up from your distractions,
Two months have passed,
And you are okay.
What is this strange feeling?
Nothing is "better", but rather, more comfortable.
You have begun your transition,
From simply existing,
To, once again,
Living.

—the physiology of grief

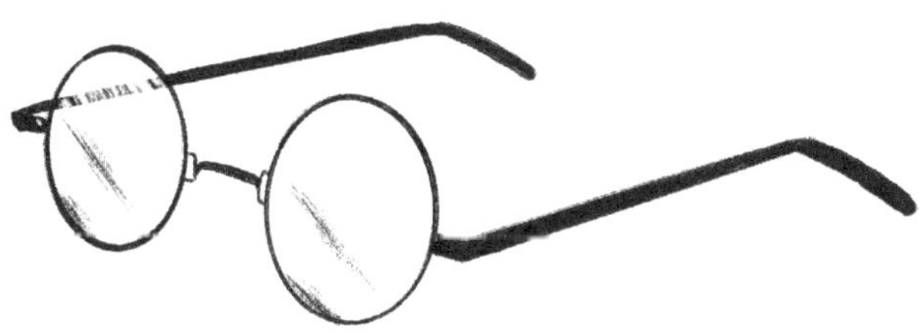

It's not your fault,
But it's your choice.

Now that you know,
—**what do you do?**

They say when someone cheats,

They aren't turning away from their partner,

They turn away from themselves.

—there are phds in this field

You said I was like the sun,
And in every hour, every room.
I would always shine for you,

My moon,
So lonely and beautiful,
Subjected to darkness every night.

Why would you turn your face
to smaller stars?
When I have always been here,
With beams of light,
Bringing warmth
into your dark sky?

—sun and moon

If I look too closely,
At any of the details,
I worry it'll become more real,
As if it wasn't real enough.

As if the truth wasn't so,

naked,
stark,
embarrassing,
horrifying,

I stare at it through my fingers,
Like a scary movie I'm compelled to watch,
But afraid to absorb.

—my least favorite genre

No grief is the same.

It is all

Immeasurable,

Organic,

And vast.

I never was able to make time,
In my own schedule,
Let alone anyone else's.

I was doing my best,
You hid your distress,
I'm sure you thought I was selfish.

The knives in the air,
Irish coffees ensnare,
Filling every second with projects.

If I didn't catch them I'd die,
A million cuts and why,
When I knew you would still reject it.

Maybe…

It wasn't even that important…
— **I know what I did**

How do I detach,
These memories,
From the physical space,
In which they occupy?

How do I remove
Ramen bowls,
Caramel lattes,
Or Fireball shots?

Dodging crowds in time square?
Tacos in the east village?
First dates on the Hudson?
Empanadas in Washington heights?

How do I take the 1 train?
Look at security guards?
Read cape comics?
Use my kettlebells?

If you can tell me how,
To enjoy regular things,
Without intrusion,
Maybe I can walk again,

Make new memories,
Seek comfort in old friends,
Turn on my music,
Mine.

And take a deep breath.
—this city is painted in your colors

Why am I being treated,
As if I was wrapped around his world?
He's the one who made me a doll in a box,
Rather than a real girl.

I've been out there all this time,
Chasing my goals,
Revising my dreams,
Ripping and resewing the seams.

So, why do people keep telling me:
"Take time for you,
Focus on yourself,
Figure out who you are."

Do they only see me from afar?

I know who I am, dammit.

Woman,
Artist,
Empath,
Daughter of Kim and Karim,

Pillar of ice,
Tower of fire,
Tears that become life-giving streams.

Storm of emotion,
Creativity to fill oceans,
Keeper of stories that gleam.

Witch, Healer,
Friend, Lover,
More than I ever seem.

And I'm not,

Fucking,

Sorry,

That I have power you'd never believe.
—a flicker

Anger

An affair,
Is a desire machine,
A place to lean,
And escape from the ring,
That you chose to hand to me,

It's a technology of sin,
Of musky skin,
An affront to kin,
Who believed the lies,
When they looked in your eyes.

Saw the truth had flown out,
Long ago,
But now,

When you admit it out loud,

Well,

—that's a place to begin

Real talk,
My blocked list,
Looks like a Blick Art Supplies receipt.

— I needed more markers anyway

Something was off,
I knew at the time,

But when I asked for reasons,
Yours always rhymed,

Who did you see?
Those months you were with me?

Said we were fine,
Just one more lie.

You smiled all the time,
Trying to cover up the crime.

You didn't try,

Or maybe didn't see,

But you had stopped talking to me,
As you delighted in her company,

Every time she blew up your phone,
—I was already alone.

I don't know who you thought I was,

But I've always been

more

—than enough.

I was the last to know,
So when I told my friends,
I didn't have to say it,

They guessed before I had a clue,
Everyone knew,
Including you,

But I still defended your name,
Defended your fame,
Defended your friendship,

You mocked me everyday,
Ripped out my heart,
Tore every sitch,

You tried to tell me what's wrong,
Where I failed,
Like I'm so heartless,

Well, I can sleep soundly at night,
I may be a fire,
But I didn't start this,

—they were your matches

Don't tell me,
I can't be angry.

At him for not protecting us,
At her for going along with it,
At people,

For being so disappointing.

Don't tell me,
I have to focus on myself.

Who do you think I am?
There isn't one thing,
I haven't been able to do,
That I have set my mind to.

Don't tell me,
He's just an asshole.

He's hurting too,
I can believe that's true,
And at least he knew,

We were on a time limit.

Don't tell me,
To calm down.

I have faced years of death,
Illness, madness, anger,
And survived,

With an education,

A job,
Friends who love me.

All for what?
For my plans to fall apart?
For one man to play me?

To treat me like a fool?

I will howl,
I'll scream and I'll cry,

I'll punch everything in sight,
Until something in my soul,
Feels alright.

—it's my turn

She got me gifts.
Random things from her job.
Sometimes for my birthday, sometimes "just 'cuz,"
Just like that,
With a cute little shrug.

"She's just like that," you said.

But I wasn't sure.
Like gifts were given as tribute.
As if she should like me,
Love me,
Because I was yours.

But...did she?

It never felt like we had a friendship.
I never felt like we needed it.

Talking to her was like talking to a predictive AI
program.
She said what she thought I wanted to hear.
But she never listened enough,
To actually get it right.

I even tested it a few times.
I didn't fault her for trying.
I just didn't care enough to correct her.

Besides....

If you did try to correct her,
She was ready,
With a list of all the reasons,
Why it's not correct to correct her.

She said it all nicely, matter-of-fact.
So you couldn't get mad.

—I never understood why

I was in a relationship with him.

—not you.

I just can't believe,
That you could go through all of this,
Assist in the creation of all this pain,
And ever think it would be worth it,

I cannot believe,
That you blame me,
For wanting to believe,
In the boy I got into this relationship with.

And yet....

And yet not blame him,
For using you,
For being twisted,
For it not working,

You may think,
I blame you more,
For trying to break us up,
It's not so,

I blame you, yes,
For being so broken,
That you put yourself in danger,
And then blamed the world for your pain,

I blame you,
For being a mistress,
And taking me to task,

As if I were the other woman,
I blame you,

For having so little respect for yourself,
That you would see our love,
And think it better to copy,
Than finding someone to call your own,

That blackmailing him,

With his own secrets and lies,
Of which you were the biggest,
Was a better alternative,
Than leaving the situation entirely,

And truly,

I blame him,
For being so weak,
That it was easier to use your company,
Than be honest with me,

I blame him,
For objectifying others,
And doing all the toxic things,
I abhor,

I blame,
And I'm not sure,
Where to go,
From blame.
—lashing out

There are so many ghosts,
I don't know every name,
But I can feel their pain,
Like blood in my veins,

It's insane,
This web,
Of conceit and lies,
And yet somehow,
I empathize,

With the way she disguised,
Her mistakes,
Like knives,
Like fodder for the beating,
Like a cycle just repeating,
New friendships for deleting,

For a price,
For a prize,
For desires left on read,
The biographies unread,
Everything she left unsaid,

Emotions undead,
Treading earth,
Bringing dread,
The baggage of the sin,
For every partner she shed,

Left unchecked,
It will be,
A hurricane of shadows,
Romance in the gallows,
A life full of hollows.

—all the hurt souls

Last time this happened,
We hadn't spoken of marriage,
There were no rings,
No long-term plans,
No future built on hollow ground,
Shaky foundations,
You knew the ground would come out from under me,
And yet you kept me,
In ignorance.

—what was the plan exactly?

In bed at age twelve,
Ticking clock kept me awake,
To cultivate myself,
No step was too large to take,
To be a better person,
Better artist,
A better student,

There wasn't a single challenge
I would have been refusing.

Fast forward:
I'm tired,
I'm hurt,
And I'm angry,

My crime?
Prioritizing my dreams,
And maybe,

I pushed you away,
But hon, you pushed me further,

Built us a life with words,
Then went and hid behind her.
the clock was always ticking

I was willing to burn,
Every bridge in my life for you.

Did you think I wasn't willing,
To burn you too?

If you crossed me?
—no way back

The words echoed,
But they didn't make sense.

You looked at me,

With the same love in your eyes,
As you sat and listed,
Every action you took,
That proved your love wasn't real.

It doesn't add up.

I can't solve for x,
When the equation is broken.
—**algebra 2**

What made it worthwhile?

Was it sweet sin?
Seductive secrets?
The rush of raw resentments?

Were her eyes pretty?

A lovely yet dull brown.
A break from the Hazel beams,
That would gaze at you with love?

Was it easy and laid back?

Did she lie for you, as she lied for you?
Tell you I demand too much,
When she'd demand nothing?

At least you both got that right.

I demand a lot.

I demand work be praised,
Not scoffed at.

I demand hands, lips,
Truth and romance.

I demand respect for who I am.
And I do not apologize for my demands.

For being a whole woman,
With hopes and plans.

—**worthiness**

I remember that day on the phone so well.

Every lie you decided to sell,
All the justifications you made,
Trying to convince yourself,
That what you did was okay,

Telling me things he didn't totally say,
Because he wasn't going to phrase it that way,
Because he said it wasn't true to how he felt,
But you wanted to keep hitting where the blow was
dealt,

Because if he really loved me,
There'd never be a you,
It's a simple concept, and yeah,
It sounds true,

You said that we were fake,
And that maybe you were the one,
But,
Do you really believe that justifies what you've done?

Because I was in the way,
Of your true love,
You wanted to see to it,
That I would give up,

But nothing you did,
Could make him give up on me,
And with work and healing,

I hoped he'd be set free,

 He did work,
And I some healing,
And I don't know,
Nor care how you are feeling,

All I know,
Is that it really is true,
You did to me,
What I could never do to you.
—but maybe I'm the bad feminist for blaming you

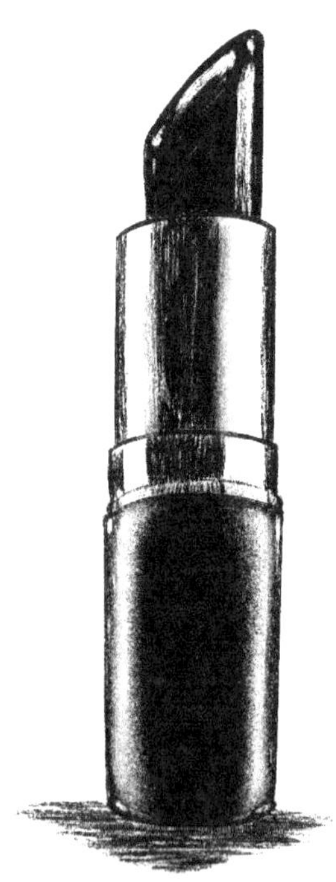

They told me I was too busy,
I didn't answer any calls.
I was building a world of magic,
So they looked too small.

It's not that I didn't love him enough,
I loved him too much to let go.
I killed myself to have it all,
To be allowed to work and grow.

And I'm not sorry I did it all,
Not sorry I worked and I strived,
Not sorry I was determined to love my life,
And...
To survive.

You can't blame me for the things you did,
You know I'm telling the truth,
When I said I would've dropped it all,
That wasn't meant just to sooth.

If only you'd been honest from the start,
If only I'd been able to see,
When you ran from yourself,
Or when you ran away from me.

I trusted you,
I would never change you,
So,

I let you leap,
Was I blind, or was your hand
Over my eyes,
So I couldn't see?

You needed to be

    In the arms of any,

    New attention.

    And did I mention?

    I knew it wasn't friendship.

I left,

Because as long as I could see your sad eyes,
I'd worry more about the fact that you're sad,
Than the fact that you caused it.

When you are in front of me,
The sound of my heart shattering,

       Is

                    distant.

I can't help it,
I learned long ago,
To tend to the hurt and injured,
Before wrapping my own bloody wounds.

—caregiver

Is there something wrong with me?
I often wonder if steel beams,
Are holding me up,
Where my bones should be,
If you cut me,
Do I bleed?
Or is it all just gasoline?
Spilling all around my feet,
So I can set fire to the sea,
Maybe then you'd understand,
What you did to me.

—demolition

You used me,

I didn't know it at the time,

But I was your tool,

Your mirror,
Your window,
The kettle to your pot,

You lashed out at me,
For having a mirrored surface,
Saw pain and malice in your reflection,
And you couldn't handle it,

Was it my education?

That I had made more of myself,
With less than your single private school expenses?

School "broke you."
Boo hoo,
I was broken too,

But I chose to gather my pieces,
To build something new,
Rather than hide them in a box,
And embark on a diatribe,
About all the reasons why,
I could no longer "try."

What did I have?

An extra degree?

A job with benefits?

A disregard for people,
Who obviously didn't understand me?

The confidence and discipline to work?
The undying optimism I could have only attained,
From almost dying?

From watching death?

Or was it his heart?
That could never be yours,
That he would rather break it over me,
Than offer you another glance?

What were you so angry about?

—your mirror

Well, you got what you wanted,

You tore us asunder,

You used my insecurity against me,

His illness against him,

Lit the fuse,

Watched the explosion,

Then cowered in the corner,

Shielding yourself from the wreckage,

 Crying to all who would listen:

"I lost my best friend, he used me, I didn't ask for this!"

Didn't you?

You came to us.

Because, I assume,

Seeking your own healthy relationship,

Would never have been as exciting,

As intruding on another's partner,
Once,

Twice,

Emotionally or physically,

As often as you could get away with.

Then you treated me like I was the other woman.

What a thrill right?

What an adrenaline rush.

What a sadistic way to medicate yourself.
—xanny is cheaper

Do you really think that I'm not focusing on myself?
That I'm waiting for you?

You think I wouldn't be standing,
If I wasn't this strong?
Wow,

—you really are full of yourself.

Don't give me your hero stories,
With villains to beat down just for glory.

Where physical strength wins the day.
Where all it takes is someone to say,
"With great power comes great—"

Yeah, okay.

Give me a hero who can push away their own fears,
In hopes of saving someone else from theirs.

Give me a hero who can stand up, and cry,
Even if their own brain tells them not to try.

Give me a hero who can put on a cape,
Even when their own fearful body quakes.

Give me a hero who wakes up each day,
Torn asunder, terrified of the fight,
Yet, finds the beauty in warm sunlight,
Finds hope in people's eyes,
Finds the kindness for themselves,
To admit they aren't okay.

And that it's okay not to be okay,
Because tomorrow is always another day.

That's true strength.
—tales of valor

I would rather be,
A silver dagger,
Sharp and small,
Glinting in the moonlight,

Than a poorly forged sword,
Dull and heavy,
Neglected,

Misused or mistaken,
For someone else's weapon.
—**weapon of choice**

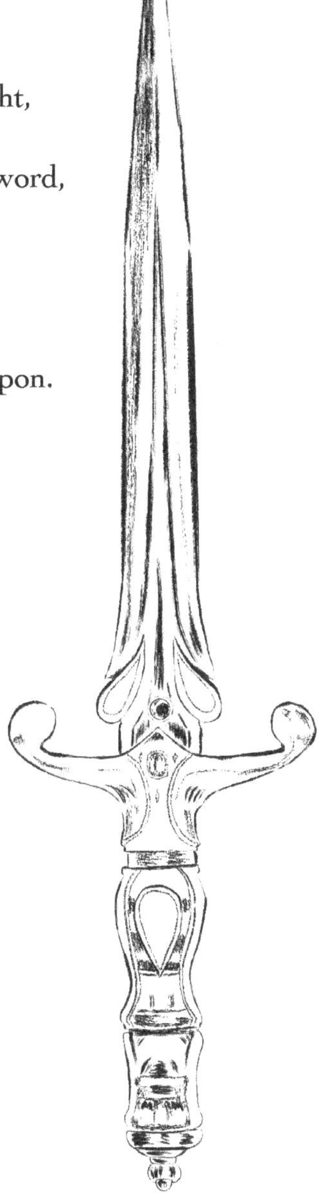

It's not the first time I trusted the wrong woman,
Over misplaced loyalty to my sex,
Intersectional regard for the feminine gender,
An allowance for the pain of patriarchy to show through,

Every woman who ever sent alarm bells ringing in my ears,
I quieted with the most empathetic words,
That,
At the time,
They didn't deserve.

"She's just broken."

"She's had a hard time."

"People have wounded and abused her."

"She is just misunderstood."

It's not that any of those statements were untrue,
To the contrary,
The details would scare you,

If you heard their tales,
Saw the scars on their hearts,
The healing wounds,
From where their bodies,
Were pried apart,

My mistake was in thinking,
That someone who had been broken by others,
Would know that pain acutely,

And would never,

Willingly,

Consciously,

Openly,

Purposefully,

Hurt another person.
—misplaced feminist instincts

To my offender,

With sparkling tears, and sad mouth,
Who has spoken to all who would listen to her woes,
I say these words with great trepidation,
With hesitation,
But declarations seem to be,
The only thing that will save me,
And so I say...

I have decided to forgive you,

But before you cry some more,
Or hurl insults,
Or tell me all the ways,
I got what I was asking for,

Hold your tongue,

And let others speak for a change.

 I decided to embrace my anger,
I engage it everyday,
A different piece,
For a different offense,

For each amount of substance I cannot understand,
I danced with my anger,
Let it engulf me,

I processed it with stamps and checks,
And then sent it on its way,
Another piece, another day,
Until there are no more left,

Until I am no longer surprised,
That you stuck needles in every eye,
That ever dared gaze kindly on me.

And still you had the gall to say,

"You weren't enough,
That's why he came my way."

"I was just doing your job for you."

So I supposed it's no wonder,
With your attitude,
That you thought you'd won,

But alas…

That prize was never yours,
It wasn't even mine,
The prize has a mind of its own.
The prize is flesh,
And blood and bone,

A human being,
Living in human time,
Which follows no logic,
No linear path,
Just the zigzagging of love,
With all its hopes and wrath,

The prize doesn't have to pick up the phone,
And, for that matter,
Neither do I,
Not when you call,

Just to pour out more lies,
And bleed my tears,
And suppress my sighs,

You'll never get this message.

Because I refuse to let you in for one more second,
And give you the chance,
To spread more manipulation,
More evil words,
That will echo til I grow deaf.

Such a sad girl,
I know you are hurt.

I'm sorry for the agony of this world.

But I didn't harm you.

My biggest crime,
Is knowing you weren't being honest,
About your true desires.

I wish you healing,
I hope whatever poison in your heart,
That could make you hurt another so,
Is eased,
And healed,
And that you are made whole.
I forgive you.

Now leave me alone.

—unsent text

I am not so serious, so boring, or unimportant,

I've got a million dreams, and darling, they are soaring,

I was never waiting for a mister and missus,

I never needed others permission,

Listen,

The mantra I wake up with every single day,

Nurture what you love, keep the chaos at bay,

when you find the one, be it person or passion,

protect them at all costs,

But don't fear confrontation.

I know,

This requires discipline,

pain, hard work,

it means you're always tired,

but you do it, 'cuz it's worth,

all the late nights, false starts,

endless second guessing,

if you want to chase your dreams,

—**darling, that's the lesson.**

Bargaining

How are we supposed to create,
If we can't even draw our demons?
How are we supposed to live,
When we are the proof our demons exist?

—a mistaken brushstroke

What must I do,
To never feel this way again?

Why did I survive,
All of the venom and drama,
Madness and illness,

Just to find myself here?
—it's been such a long road, and I am tired.

Have you always been two people?
A cliche version of an evil twin?
Dark intent knocking at the door,
Waiting to be let in?

Or are you like two souls
in one body?
Never knowing which one
is true,

Hiding sickness,
One suffocating the other,
A constant dance,
Fighting for control,

Both crying out to be whole?
—**inner struggle**

I

    was

        trying

            to be honest,

With myself,

About all the ways,
I ignored cries for help.

I did let her in,

I did turn my back,

In not wanting to fight,
I ignored the attacks.

I don't blame myself,
This isn't my fault.

You made these choices.

This wasn't my call.

But I can't say,
"I tried everything."

That hurts worst of all.

—reflection pt. i

Though I believe in love,
Sometimes it's not enough.

It's not that I need a relationship,
I just want you here.
Even if it causes me tears.
—I don't know how to love halfway

I get scared when I think,

"He's not mine."

But that's not totally true,

Because he was never his own either.

We all need to be our own first,

Or we can never be someone else's.
—on being whole

Why should I change?
Be less kind?
Pull back my love, reserve my time?

Why shouldn't I give others the benefit of the doubt?

It does hurt,
Being let down,
Waves of disappointment resound.

But why does that mean I should only expect worse?

My father would say:
"Thank God we still think well enough of people
To be surprised by their dark deeds."

—stubbornness

"Resentment is ridiculous."
—**a good friend pt. i**

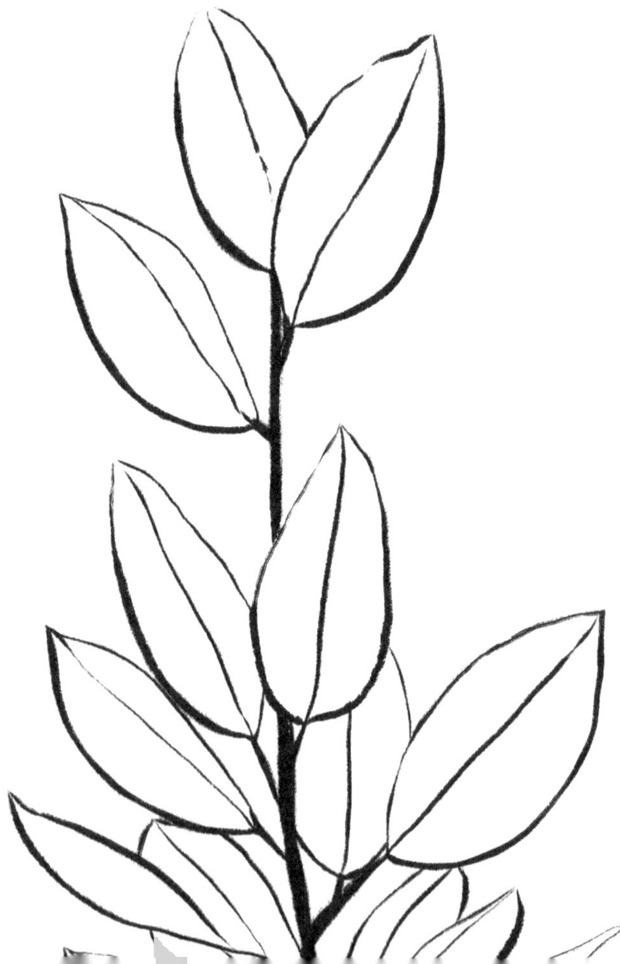

What a horror show it is in our bodies.

When our illness causes us,
To become people we never knew.

Am I my worst moments?

Are you your best ones?

Or is it this tightrope,
That we tread,
With trembling feet,
Somewhere in between.

That defines who we are?

—**messy**

When I told you she said,
"I was doing your job for you,"
You recoiled from your screen.

Your work chair rolling you back,
Deeper into your Queens apartment,
As you reeled, half-laughing in full-horror,
Yelling "you made that up!"

There were tears in my eyes,
From laughing so hard,
My sides ached,
It felt so great to smile.

You shook your head at the mere thought,

Marveled at the gall of the other woman,

Reminded me I was loved,

And bribed me with future plans
To picnic by our beloved river,
With warm food and frozen drinks,

You gave a little piece of myself,
Back to me.

I'll always be grateful for that.
—a good friend pt. ii

I don't know why I'm like this.

I don't know how I could be so hurt,
With so much pain in me,
Yet still free.

I don't know why,
When I see you,
I can't help but smile.

My friends want me to be angrier.
But I can't,
Not this time.
—don't ask me why

How many nights did I lay here,
Wrapped in any blanket I could find,
Reading books of poetry,
Touching the words on the page,
Hoping they can save me,
Answer the questions that gnaw away at me,
Give me hope for future of joy?

Those poets were my friends,
My misery's favorite company,
A lifeline in the void,
A constant reminder,

    That if nothing else,
    We create.

        In the depths of pain,
        We build worlds.

        With our agonized cries,
        We breath life,

            And that the teardrops we shed,
            Can be used to paint truths.

    —time passed

Can I help loving you?
That I believed in what we had.
That the thought of seeing you fills me with painful joy.
That, for so many days,
You were my smile.

Can I help being angry?
That you threw me away,
That you made another more important,
That you abandoned all our plans,
Brought an end to all our happiness.

For what?

Can I help crying?
Over the image you had of me,
Some cold and angry girl.
Cold because you left me shivering.
Angry because you had hurt me before.
Now in pain because she's still in love with you?

Can I help being numb?
Because I ripped out my heart,
Gave it to you and said:
"Fine, but please, don't break it again."

And what did you do?
Took that heart,
Buried it in glass shards,
Let others throw darts at it,

Dissected it like a frog in biology class.

Why?

Can I help drowning?
Because you didn't tell me the ice was breaking,
Not until it was too late,
Not until I was falling through the cracks.
I had just enough time,
My will to live encased me,
Floated me just above the water,
I drifted away.

To safety?
To new beginnings?
To your arms?
Or another's?

Can I help being afraid?

—can I help being hopeful?

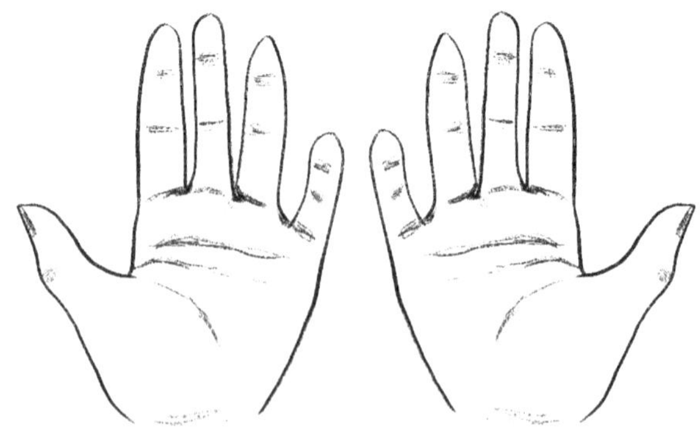

As each day goes by,
It grows more difficult not to speak to you.

I want to lay on your chest,
And open my heart.

Unveil every truth.

Unpack every lie.

Find out where I still fit into your world,
If I fit at all.

I want you to be honest,

To be the sweet one I knew,
Who cried for me, and never hung up first.

Who was by my side,
When my father died.

Let's take this thing apart,
Look at every angle,
See if it's worth another try.

If I'm honest,

You're the only one
I want in my life.

But you can't stay,
Unless you'll work to make it right.

I can love you,
Without compromise.
—thoughts at night

Is it your fault you're broken?
That people broke you?

Or is it your fault that you didn't get help,
When you sorely needed it?

Is it my fault for loving someone,
With an illness?

Is it my fault for being understanding,
Of the illness?

Is it your fault that I'm broken?
Or mine for letting you break me?

—**blame,** **blame,** blame

Limerence,
Is a state of mind,
A romantic attraction,
Confusing relation,
Fiery obsession,
A painful situation,

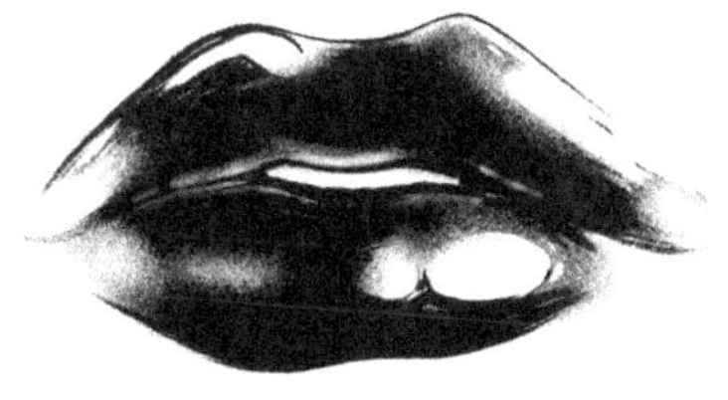

A prolonged vacation,
A cheap motel,
Your partner's shadow,
Where you can't tell,
When you crossed the line,

Or why,

You aren't stopping,
The mountain of lies,

Because this is an attraction,
To the-lesser-than person,
To a lack of responsibility,
To the one who asks nothing.

Nothing but a state of mind,
An empty relationship,
A partner-less partnership,
No smoke in that hit,

Limerence,
is a fantasy,
Where no one gets hurt,
No effort is made,
And animal instinct is enough.

—look it up

Who were we in 2013?

Kids,

With innocent feelings,
That led to indecent meetings.

Mere children at 21 and 23.

Still believing in true love,
Despite our own obstacles.

The world's barrage.

The arrows of slights aimed at us.

Dodging bullets,

Exiled,

Hurting ourselves and each other.

Misunderstood by most,
Invalidated by those we trust,

"We didn't stand a chance."

Love may defeat all,
But it still leaves you battle weary.
—**it survives,**
      but barely

How many days was it?

It seems like a hundred,
But maybe it was only three.

Before my body,
Gasping for art,
For inspirational release,

Pulled me to my desk.

Kicking and screaming,
Cursing my fate,
forced me to create.
—gifted

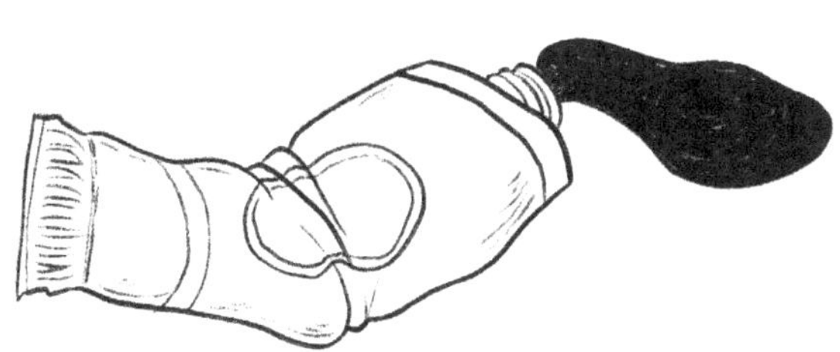

It's painful work,
Turning this mess into art,
Weaving,
This incomprehensible tangle of hurt,
Into one tapestry of emotion.

Could you at least hand me the loom?
The needles? The pins?
Could you lend me the string?
The one I wrapped around your arms,
Each loop another story, a memory,
A little more pain,

Let me wind it into a ball,
Into something useful,
Something I can create with,
Instead of something that trips me,
Whenever I dare smile.

—**crying creatively**

Depression

I create constantly for the eyes of others,
So when this started pouring out of me...

Like a dam,
        flooding,
                cracking,
                        breaking,

I couldn't contain it,
I couldn't cling.

As words overflow,
Like an undertow,

Sweeping me out to sea.

The truth will out,
Whether I like it or not.

And this work is much bigger
and more unruly than me.
—none of this was meant to be seen

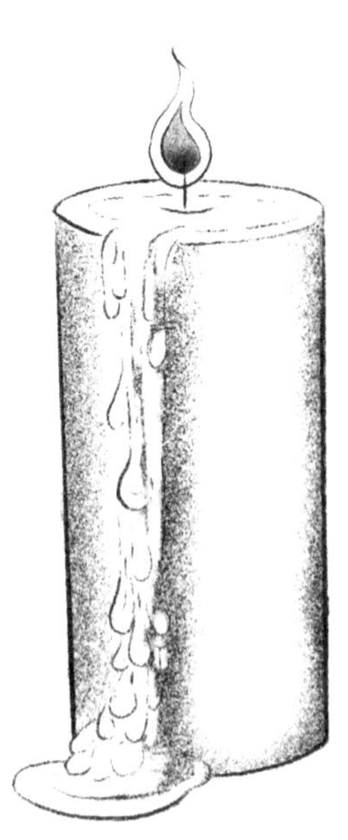

No poetry,
No pretty words,
I'm just tired of being sad,

Plain and simple.

I just want to exist,

My body felt,
As though it had been poisoned.

Days went by,
Unable to keep anything down.

Then suddenly,
It stopped.

And now I just want to sleep.
—**weariness**

In the midst of a year,
Where nothing feels as important,
As stopping a deadly virus,
I still managed to cry a river of tears over you,

—pandemic year

In the darker moments,

Between the bitter words and whiskey glasses,

I wonder if I'll be my own destruction,

Making things madly,
Sharing with no one,
Finishing nothing,

Always healing just enough to be shattered again,

But never enough to be whole.
—**artist**

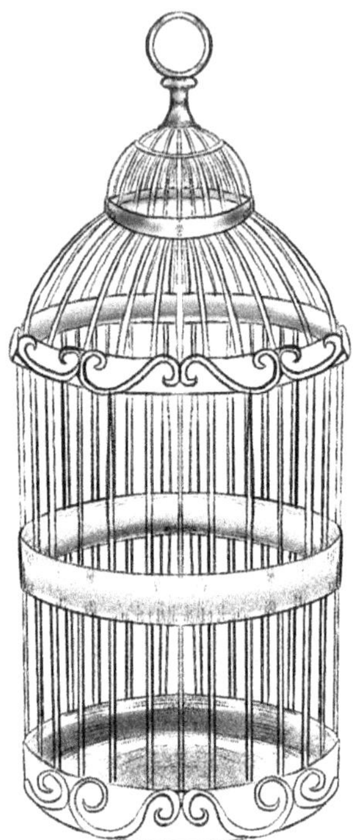

I was imprisoned
in unchecked bitterness,
Crying for help,
But no one could rescue me
from my own cage.

You may have built the cell.
        But I
                took the key,
                        I'm the one
                                who locked
                                        the door.

—prison

I've gotten so used to working with lumps in my throat.

Looking at me,
I'm a typical 9-5.

But in my head,

I'm standing on fragments of glass,
Afraid to cut my feet.

Fire raging around me,
Yet too cold to move my trembling fingers faster.

Somehow I'll survive this.
One breath at a time.

—can't quit my day job

When I see old pictures of myself,
My eyes burn,
My throat closes,
Seeing the smiling girl.

Because I feel so sorry,

She thought the world was her oyster,
And her relationship was safe.
Thinking the worst thing that could happen,
Already did.

What else would you think,
After you've lost a parent?

Not realizing the cruelty,
Hurtling at high speed,

The manipulation and shit-talk,
Cannon ready.

That my enemies had disguised themselves as friends.

And that you were the Trojan horse.

—past self

And yet...

No matter how much pain I'm in...

When I look up at the sky tonight,

And smile at the moon and stars,

—I hope you're looking at it too.

I'm afraid of you.
I'm afraid you'll get tired of me.
I'm afraid I'll prove your worst assumptions correct.
I'm afraid I'll become the angry girl you painted me as.
I'm afraid you'll judge me.

Even though,
            You're,

                        The,

                                    One,

                                                who…

I am not afraid of fire.
I am not afraid of judgement.
I am not afraid of failure.
I am not afraid of anyone.

—12am mantra

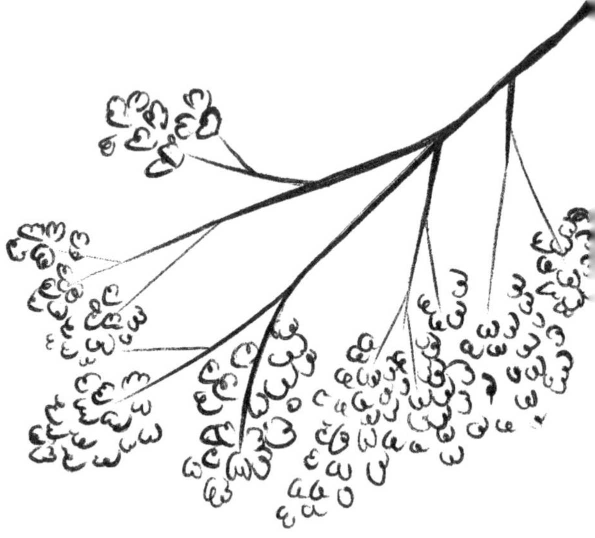

I never was able to forgive on my own schedule,
—**let alone anyone else's.**

The "daily word" my mother reads,

Said: "forgiveness sets me free".

And that was the first time I started to believe,

The universe truly was guiding me.

A power,

A ghost,

A friendly hand,

Lukewarm,

Hardly there,

Except at 2am.

When music vibrates my weary heart,

Some power dragging me to bed,

So I can wake up in the morning,

And try, try, try again.
—four days after the revelation

Every day is an eternity,
Every hour a test of skill.
What was so important?
Where did I get the will?

I'll admit I wanted everything,
But Chronos was never on my side,
The clock was ticking so endlessly,
It took my focus, it took my life.

A job,

Degrees,

Financial stability,

None of it matters
Without you with me.

Now even as my heart is breaking,
I'm still wishing you were here.
Hold me close and tell me, "everything's alright,"
Oh honey,
  —please erase my fears.

They will ask you for forgiveness,
Beg you, and plead.
But you didn't choose,
Any of their deeds,

They will call you angry,
Say your heart is too hard.
But they caused the wounds.
That turned into painful tight scars,

You can't simply forgive them,
Before the time has come.
Not before they try to erase,
What it is they have done.
—you must forgive on your own time

I want to live,
not just exist.

I learned to listen,
To the sound of my own heartbeat.

The rhythm was reliable,
Like steady waves,
In calm waters.
—**still in my boat**

One day you wake up,

You don't immediately think something is wrong,

You calmly go about your morning,

Wash your face,

Put on clothes,

Drink something warm,

There's a sadness,

Sitting in the back of your head,

But today it's okay,

There are other things to do,

Time marches on.

—daily routines

Even on perfect mornings,

When the sun shines through my window,
Steam rising from a fresh cup,
As I light my rose-scented candle,
My mind starts to wonder,

To another thought of you with them,
To those you called friends,
To all the romantic things,
That should have stayed between you and me,

I don't try to picture your indiscretions,
I'd be remiss if I didn't mention,
Every horror movie I refused to see,
Because I have an overactive imagination.

I take a deep breath, I meditate,
When you've been shattered you get great,
At recognizing the cliff's edge,
Before it's far too late.

Slowly this is starting to feel like a reconnection,
So I suppose it's time for another session,
To truly heal from this discretion,
And slowly wiggle out of this depression.

—one page at a time

When I was a little girl,
I prayed every day,
For someone to love me,
I wanted to find a way,

For my hero to fly in,
And make it all better,
Pen running on paper,
I wrote a thousand letters,

One day, I got an answer,
A breath of wind had crossed the sea,
Delivering a piece of salt stained paper,
It was signed, "future me."

—**a sudden note**

Dear Friend,

       I hope this letter finds you well, although I know how you feel these days.

       What you don't know is that things are about to change for the better. I am so proud of you. You got to work. You wrote again for the first time in years, you got back to your art, you started a side-hustle to keep your mind busy, you mapped out the long-forgotten dreams you had. You started therapy again, and stuck to it, you reached out to friends, and you still made time to listen to others.

       It's all going to pay off, dear one. Sooner than you realize, it's going to be okay. Know that in the future, you/I am surrounded by love. We waited for the right type of love, for honest and open love, and our faith was rewarded. We never stopped working on our goals, and we prioritized them. We started to think about what kind of life we wanted, and focused our energy. We built our career and we have so much art, and peace, and safety in our lives in a way that seemed impossible before.

       You are so hardworking. You've never wavered. We've caused ourselves a lot of trouble with that soft heart, but that's what made our art good, our stories real, our energy warm. We had so much power, and we still do.

       You're such a lucky, strange, lovely person. Don't be discouraged. Don't give up on yourself. Don't drive yourself crazy over them either. Don't worry about anyone else.

You have PLENTY of work to do.
Dive into it.
Enjoy it.

       I love you, my sweet little past self. You're trying so hard. I'll be cheering for you. See you soon.

Love,

—your future self.

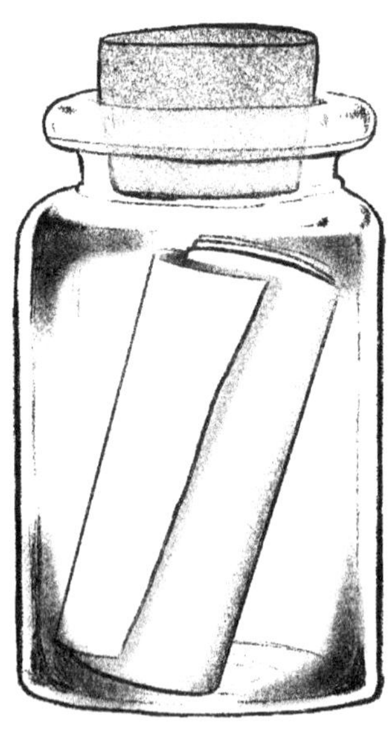

Reconnection

He's going to love me so much more when he's sober from
all this bull***t

They say God doesn't give you anything you can't handle,
Well, I asked God if I could phone a friend,
My friend picked up and like a soothsayer, said,
"It's as if you were made for this."

Damn...

Like someone could be made to handle betrayal,
Coping skills forged from the finest steel,
Still I couldn't say it wasn't true.
I'm anxious, depressed, but certainly not frail.

—stronger than I thought

I would have drowned,

Over,
And over,
And over,
In all the tiny,
Broken,
Things.
—I couldn't live like that anymore

It took me one week,
To finally break our silent streak,
Anger fueled my hurried fingers as I dialed you,
Ready for more disappointment and denial.

My mouth snapped shut when you told me:
You enrolled yourself in recovery,
And since the day I left,
You'd been attending meetings.

No offense,
But honestly,

I had to see it to believe.

I didn't think you were strong enough to do that.

You were a lot of talk sometime,
You didn't want to be, but you were,
It's fine.

I was used to that default,
But that wasn't what I found when I called.
—you actually got help

People will not always hold space for you.
—you must hold space for yourself

I know I'll be okay.
I'm me.
—I'm one of the strongest people I know.

Thank god for friends.

Bless their warmth,
Their concerned eyes,
Their loving jokes,
And their ability to know,
Your favorite food and drink.

Bless the grass.
On which we laugh.

As I unfold my heart to them,
They look at me with love and understanding.
I know they're mad at you.
But they hold most of it back.
Sensing it would cause me to come to your defense.

They hold space for me.

My worries,
My tears,
My anger,
My depression,

And most importantly,

—my hope

On a picnic blanket,
You both waited,
With sushi and cider.

I expected a funeral for my heart,
Hurting and tender.
But instead, you celebrated life.

Toasted,
To my ability to love.

Told me,
"All good things start with you."

Treated me,
Like a shining star in the summer sky.

We drank bubbly things under the setting sun,
We looked at stars and talked about music,
You gave pieces of myself back to me,
One by one,

In this way,
I became whole again.

—soothing bonds

How can you be the one who made me feel homeless,
And yet still be my home?

How can you be the reason I was in survival mode,
For months,
And yet, make me feel safe?

—a contradiction

I now know he loves me,

Still,

Despite it all.

He's fighting to get better,

To be stronger,

And work out his own issues.

Just in case,

I decide to come back.

So now,

It is pain without fear,

We are truly tearing it down,

Stripping this relationship,

Of any facade.
—no more cheap scaffolding

How can I be someone who believes in change?

Who looks in the mirror,
Proud of my own growth,
Who waters plants,
To see new life spring forth,
And not see the change he gained?

How can I ignore the work?

The empty pens,
Pages and pages of documentation,
Painful timelines,
Brutal confessions,
Risking over and over my disgust?

Disdain,
Mistrust,
Workshops,
Lessons,
Still doing sessions,

Hoping,
I'll feel safe enough,
To let him back in.

— it's a little hard to believe

Another day goes by,
Another piece falls out,
Causing more waves of pain.

But these days you're here to answer my cries.

You pick up the pieces,
Glue them back into place,
Another damaged section, repaired, replaced.

You've been helping me glue for weeks now.

How thankful should I be,
When you were the one who shattered me?

—keep repairing

I have no desire to remain on a sinking ship.

No desire to stay with someone,
Who would rather grieve over the holes in the hull,
Than leap out and swim to safety.

No desire to suffocate in this icy sea.

When this truth washed over me,
It knocked me off my feet.
My survival instincts kicked in,

I swam to shore.

I built a boat from broken promises.
Fashioned a canvas with hope for my future.
I sailed away,

I saved myself.

And as I turned for one final farewell, what did I see?
The one who once would have rather cried his plea,
Had built his own boat, just to catch up to me.

    —sailing

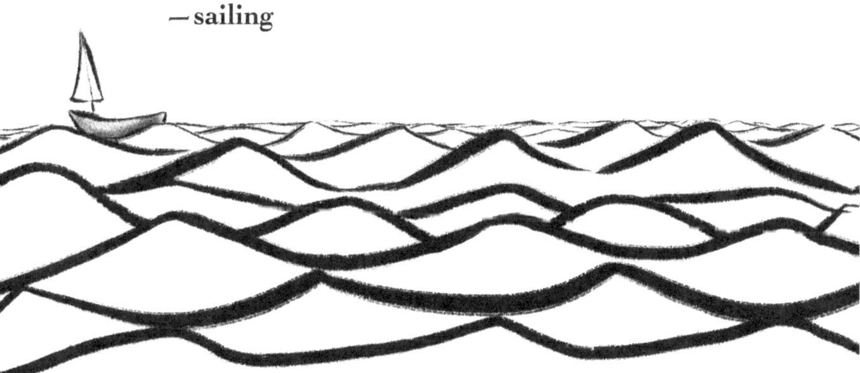

"I want to be the boy you fell in love with."

Is it possible to become clean after something like this?

To scrub away all the thoughts previously unthinkable?

The flowering stains of sin and revelation,
The reeling,

     Metallic,

         Slick,

            Sticky flecks,

Covering your skin,
Blocking sound and sight,
Filling what was once benign with a sense of dread.

— I keep running out of soap

99.9 percent is not you,
You didn't choose it,
To feel like a fool,
To feel like a habit, quit.

But that 00.1 is haunting,
A cold hand on your cheek,
No amount of anger,
Could make it less bleak,

Truthfully you knew,
Something was amiss,
The kisses were the same,
The dates were still bliss,

But something wasn't right,
Like the faintest mist,
What you didn't ask was screaming,
From your heart's abyss.

—it happened on your watch

I…
was,
trying,
to be honest,
with myself.

About all the ways,
I ignored cries for help.

When I saw the therapy receipt,
The mantras,
The rituals,
The daily meetings,

The way you coped with yourself,
The explanations,
The conversations,
Every answer to my questions,

Your hurt,
Your confusion,
That my pain,
You regretted,

Your slow words,
Careful thoughts,
Trying to show me,
To support my healing.

It made it easier to look
At my own two hands,

My plans,
My bitterness,
My anger,
My revenge,

My hurt,
My bruises,
My fears,
And my friends,

To be honest about,
The way I had been,
The things I hated,
In my own soul's den.

So why am I here?
Why did I call?
Because I had to know,
I gave it my all.
—reflection pt. ii

What will it take,

To make the good times good again?

To remove the bitter taste?

To feel as happy as we should again?
—**I just saw old pictures of us**

Today,
Is the first morning,
Since the last morning,
Of our previous life.

The sun spills through our window,
Liquid light filtering into gold,
Illuminating the dark corners,
Showing the debris that still needs to be swept.

There's so much shrapnel from the burst,
I still find them in my limbs,
Those sharp pains in my arm,
As I reach for my pen.

The sound of your breath makes me chest tight,
I can't comprehend,
How a human can cause so much pain,
Yet sleep so soundly,
Looking as sweet as the boy I saw you for.

My mind is buzzing,
The remnants of adrenaline,
Like a guardian angel,
Asking me over and over,

"Why are we here?"

We're here because there is less debris.
We're here because my scars are healing.
We're here because he wanted to change.
We're here so we could make it safe again.

One beam of fresh wood,
To make a new foundation,
On a clear plot of land,
For an honest do-over.

—october air

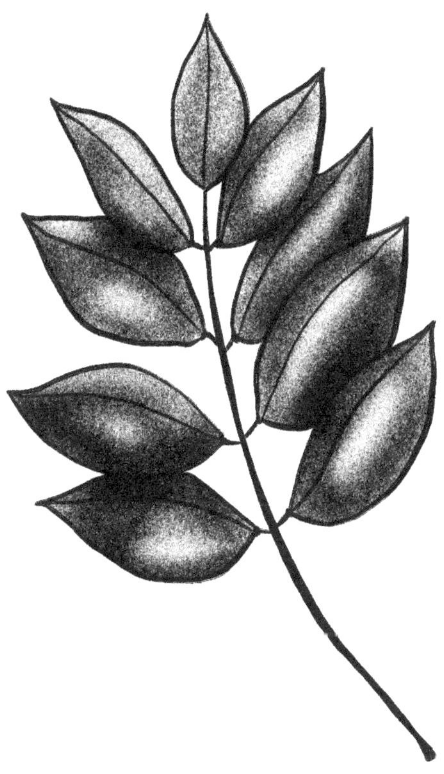

Acceptance

I always thought,

That I was the one,

Who created the work.

Who wrote the words,

Who moved the pencil,

Who drew the face.

Who painted the piece.

How naive was I?

I couldn't see.

That it was the work,

That was creating me.
—living sketchbook

I was not safe, you see,
In my own mind,
There were too many broken things,
That I had simply boxed away,

The boxes spilled open,
I cut myself on their contents,
By accident, by carelessness,
By a desire to only be in pain,

I wanted to wear my sorrow,
But it would have suffocated me,
I hid it with liquor and love,
With empty promises,
And broken touches.

—I know this now

Please don't grow cold,
Don't seal off your soul,

You don't need to harden,
To survive this world,

—it's the world that should soften for you

Glance this way,

I'll hold your gaze,

Like I did the first day,

You ever laid,

>   Your pretty eyes,

>   On my face,

>   **—back to the beginning**

I wanted them to stop taking you away from yourself.

Not me.
—**yourself.**

It started with his gestures, you know?

When he started making moves,
That rebuilt not destroyed,
That healed, not hurt.

He made it easier,

To choose our happiness,
Over his damage,
And my bitterness.
—**it is possible**

"You're the one that saw,
That I was letting myself waste away."

"You pushed me every day,
To be the me,
you knew I could be."
—he said

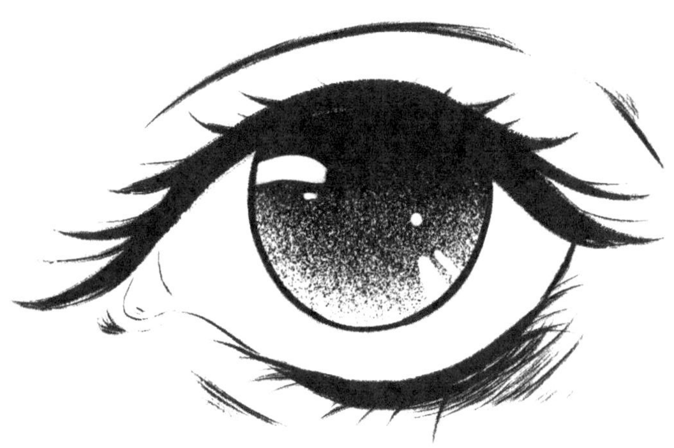

We have one shot at life.
For that I am grateful.

Life is too precious to waste,
On sadness,
Hatred,
Or shame.

I will live with my head high,
My heart soft and strong,

My mind clear.

The future is mine,
The rest is a detail.

—no more moping

The colors of the holiday lights blurred,
As tears filled my eyes.

With concern in your voice you asked,
What's wrong?

I said:
"I never thought I'd see the lights,
With your hand in mine,
Ever again."

You smiled.

—but you got teary-eyed too

What helps the most,
Is that for every shock,
You pause and check in,
You backtrack and reassure,
You understand it's not me,

It's ptsd.

You're trying to understand,
You read books and you plan,
You take my hand,
And take a stand,
We're becoming best friends.
—once again.

Our bodies are miracles,

The very things that you swear,

Will push you to an early grave,

Wind up being,

The very ashes you rise from,

As glorious as a Phoenix,

Coated in the euphoria of survival,

And the peace of newfound safety.
—**cleansing fire**

Don't spend so much time on people,
Who won't be more than a footnote,
In the history of your life.

—note to self

We are forged by the things,
That did not defeat us.

By the imperfect circumstances,
We worked around.

By the crisis and contentment,
To get through it.

By the muscles we grew,
When our old ones were torn,

Because to survive,
We had to go on.

—inner strength

As your mistakes fade,
I remember the good.

Whenever I felt down,
Or when my dreams seemed too far,
You'd remind me how much closer,
They now are.

Even when my heart aches,
For goals I haven't reached,
You would smile at me,
Take my hand, kiss my cheek.

You marked down all my steps,
Every turn and achievement,
You remind me that I'm strong,
"Don't you give up on your dreams yet."

This cheerleader, hope-bringer,
This soft, supportive guy,
The one I've dated all these years,
Under every season's sky.

The one who understood,
Who saw me as a candle in the wind,
Burning bright, threatening to go out,
You shielded me and grinned.

The one who stands,
—by my side

The worst part,
Of life threatening pain,
Is the art,
That pours like rain.

The best part,
Of life threatening pain,
Is the art,
That pours like rain.

— destruction/salvation

You were coming home from training.
But geo-location placed you at the gym.
It didn't make sense, and I panicked,

Was this about to happen again?

When you got home, I admitted my fears,
Asked "were you actually there? Alone?"
You apologized, let me have that moment.

"Next time" you said,
 "I can take a pic on my phone."

Proof,

Is what you constantly offer,
I worry there can never be enough.
These months you're unwaveringly honest,
And we both know...

I could tell if you bluffed.

You didn't blame me for my paranoia,
I didn't blame you for the past,
This is how we can move forward,
Healing and talking, so this can last.

—healthy communication styles

We sat in the same spot,
As that July weekend.

A Saturday,

So different,

In every conceivable way.

We spoke about our plans,
Our future,

Real again,

An apartment with sunlight,
A few plants,
To give us the oxygen,
And solar power we need,
To live and breathe free,
From the shadows we flee.

That day long past,
We sat by the river,
And spoke about a "what-if" future,
Where you somehow healed,
And I stopped hurting,
Long enough to rebuild together.

Someday,

Maybe,

Was it possible?

Unclear.

But at some point you decided,

"What if" had to be "when."

You got the help you needed,
To be a better partner, and friend.

So.

Now we're here,
Sitting by the river,
again.

—a way forward

After years of lies,

She still cared for me.

Her eyes,
Red,
Tear-soaked,
Filled with fear,

Despite it all,

She still was kind to me.
                    With a gentle grace,
                        She walked away,

with hope that one day,
I would repair myself,
But,
It would have to be alone.

These character flaws,
Engrained so deep.
Deception,
Addiction,

But now I see,

Honesty,
Consistency,
Rebuilding "me".

For the day that "me",
Is once again "we".

I can't erase my past sins,
But I can rebuild.

Take this first step.

Move forward, still,

—one day at a time.

Healing

I would not wish my misfortunes,
On my worst enemies,

But I wouldn't trade,
The infinite joy of surviving,
For a more peaceful past either.

I was so mad,
At my hopeful past self,
For thinking the best,
And trying to help,

So sad for that girl,
So sincere,
While her loved ones played,
On her very worst fears,

Now I see her with love,
And I'm glad for her heart,
Bleeding but succeeding,
Not torn clean apart.
—she was doing whatever she could

Some nights I want to cry,
Not from sorrow,
But from the deepest gratitude,
For my life,

—I'm so glad I am here.

The smaller me,

I want to kiss her tiny forehead,

Hand her the best tools,

Listen to her dreams over and over,

Tell her what a great job she's doing,

Sweet thing,

I wish I could wrap you in a wing,

Make you a warm drink,

Croon low tunes,

Rock your weary body to sleep,

Somehow make you believe,

You'd be okay.

— I'm so proud of you

Your brain is abuzz,
Like fireflies reminding you there's light,
Like the hum of a laptop processing new data,
Like a blinking cursor on a blank page,
Full of great and terrible possibilities,

There are too many thoughts,
Too much to sort through,
Infinitely possible places,
An endless mountain of to-dos,
But life doesn't stop,
—and neither do you

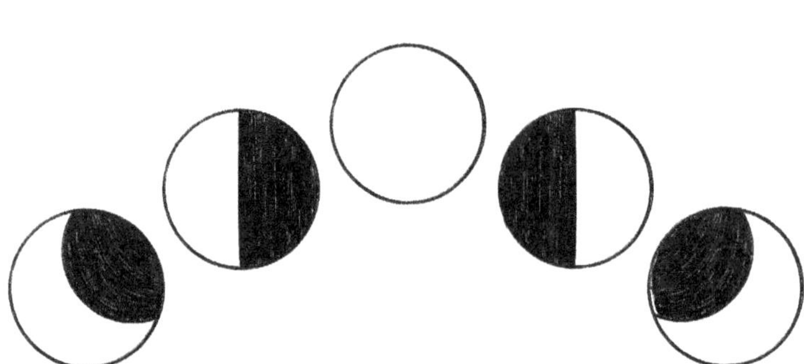

When you're afraid,
Light it up, it's a day,
It's just a minute away,
From you being okay,

I know it's true,
Because I was once you,
Feeling buried and beaten,
Heart battered and bruised,

If you look closely,
With nothing more to lose,
You can see the scars healing,
You can walk in their shoes,

Believe it or not,
It was never about you,
Often this happens,
They have no clue,

The tearing, the burning,
The hole punched clean though,
But life will go on,
So what will you do?

Whatever your choice,
Time will leave you behind,
Make every moment count,
And sooth your mind,

I promise dearest,
You will be just fine.
—believe me, my friend

When you are frozen,
Move.
When you are speechless,
Sing.
When you are hurting,
Write.
When you are crying,
Draw.

It doesn't matter what comes out.
Doesn't matter,
If it's a masterpiece,
Or simply a mark,

Turn your pain into art.
—**coping mechanisms**

So many pieces,
Every corner, everywhere,
It isn't right, isn't fair,
The debris of the memories we shared,

Pick them up, and lay them out,
Pour hot liquid between the cracks,
One by one, it comes back together,
Something new that can last,

It's not a fast process, no magic pill,
You have to be patient,
Sit with it, be still,
Smooth the pieces into place, have no regrets,
Feel every emotion from every sharp edge.

Wherever you are, whatever you choose,
You'll be so happy that despite what you knew,
All the dark times, and all the pain,
You put it back together, with grace, without blame,

Forgive each shard,
Bless each piece,
If you stay in anger,
You'll have no relief,

Once again whole,
Complete with gilded rivers,
Tracing the journey,
That brought you thither.

Through shock, denial, anger, and tears,
Bargaining, depression, reconnection, through years,
You're here and now, or soon you will be,
With gold in your heart for all to see.

—repair it with gold

When you make something happen,

With your own two hands,

You scare the demons away,

And make it more difficult,

For them to burrow into your heart,

And stay there.
—**hard won advice**

It feels like death,
But they aren't dead.

Or are they?

Something always dies.

Your image of them,
Of your partnership,
The world you thought you knew,
The memories you thought you had.

Whether you stay and rebuild,
Or leave and heal yourself,
You will always be mourning something.

And that's okay,
I promise it is,
Whatever your decision,
I'll be there to stand with you,
—at the wake

You will certainly forgive,

And you must,
For your own sake,

But please understand,
Forgiveness is not the same as permission,

You will not forgive for them.
You will forgive for you.

You don't need to condone anything,
You don't need to understand why,

You don't need to "get" it,
You only need to see broken things for their pieces,

Understand that it is broken,
Take pity on its sharp edges,

And forgive.

Forgive him for hurting you,

Forgive her for hurting you,

Forgive them for hurting you,

Forgive yourself for getting hurt.

—you deserve forgiveness the most

After the hurting,

The releasing,

The healing,

You'll be so relieved.

Relieved you held on,

Relieved you tried,

Relieved you didn't stop,

Relieved you're still here.
—letters to broken people

To my editor,
Who showed me the limitless possibility,
Of consistent friendship,
Combined with persistent work,
Ever-loving and honest.

Without you,
These poems would never have,
The sun on their face,
They would have lived,
In the shadow of a doubt,
Instead of a warm place,
With my most trusted first reader,
And a true friend.

—**thank you**

Printed in the United States of America

First Printing Spring 2022

Paperback ISBN: 978-0-578-37058-3
Ebook ISBN: ISBN 978-0-578-37059-0

Edited by Haley Spaeth
Interior Design by Kam Peck
Cover Design by Samia Fakih

Smudge Studios
New York, NY
10032

www.SamiaSelene.com